# Grandma's Love

### Adeleine "Addie" Mayo

ISBN 978-1-0980-4930-0 (paperback)
ISBN 978-1-0980-4931-7 (digital)

Christian Faith Publishing, Inc.
832 Park Avenue
Meadville, PA 16335
www.christianfaithpublishing.com

Printed in the United States of America

To Lana and Lyric
In fond memory of Grandmother Mary

The joyous times we spent at Grandma's
fills my heart with praise.

She always made us cakes and fed
us foods we loved to eat.

Her tender, loving, caring ways made
our stay with her complete.

Gently she'd correct us during
the many times we fought.

We learned to love each other through
the lessons we were taught.

"Train up a child in the way
he should go, and when he
is old, he will not turn from it."

Proverbs 22 : 6

She'd always take us places where
we'd have lots of fun—

to parks and recreation areas,
outdoors where we could run.

It seemed she knew just what to do
for every hurt and bruise.

The hurt would be forgotten with
the remedies she'd use.

I never saw her angry or
upset or torn apart.

A calm and quiet soul she seemed
to be, a true sweetheart.

"Prosperity will serve him; future generations
will be told about the Lord. They will proclaim
his righteousness to a people yet unborn - for
he has done it."

Psalm 22:30, 31

We'd always want to stay at Grandma's house another night.

Whenever Mom would pick us up,
the time was never right.

We'd plead with Mom, "Just one more night, please, will you let us stay?"

And Grandma always helped us out;
she knew just what to say.

When the fun was finally over, and
we knew we had to go,

in loving hugs and kisses her affection for us showed.

The Lord's always been with Grandma;
in her sweet heart he abode.[1]

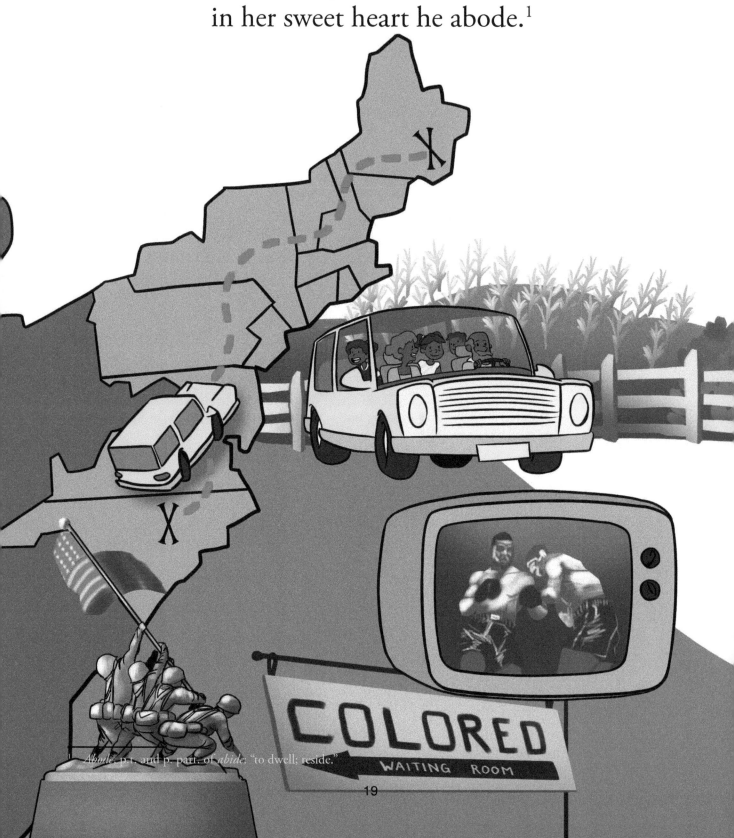

[1] *Abode*: p.t. and p. part. of *abide*: "to dwell; reside."

I believe He's traveled with her through
a long and winding road.

When I reflect on my childhood,
I thank our Lord above

for fond memories of the blessings of a childhood filled with Grandma's love.

# About the Author

Adeleine "Addie" Mayo is an educator of young children with a Master of Science degree in mathematics education from Simmons College.

Out of her love for people, family and intergenerational connectedness, Addie has written this children's book as a legacy to her children and her children's children of a childhood filled with the love of a grandmother.

Addie desires to restore the concept of honor between children and parents and grandchildren and grandparents and throughout the extended family through the remembrance of unconditional love expressed from one generation to another.

She gives honor to God the Father, the Lord Jesus Christ and Holy Spirit who has shed his love abroad in our hearts and given those of us who believe an unlimited capacity to love and to forgive.

CPSIA information can be obtained
at www.ICGtesting.com
Printed in the USA
BVHW050924200421
605396BV00010B/2147

9 781098 049300